W9-ATO-901

I Can Make

ART

written and photographed by

Mary Wallace

Owl Books

I Can Make Art

Owl Books are published by Greey de Pencier Books Inc.,
370 King St West, Suite 300, Toronto, Ontario M5V 1J9

Owl and the Owl colophon are trademarks of Owl Communications.
Greey de Pencier Books Inc. is a licensed user of trademarks of Owl Communications.

Distributed in the United States by Firefly Books (U.S.) Inc.,
230 Fifth Avenue, Suite 1607, New York, NY 10001.

This book was published with the generous support of the Canada Council,
the Ontario Arts Council and the Government of Ontario through
the Ontario Publishing Centre.

Cataloguing in Publication Data

Wallace, Mary, 1950–
I can make art

ISBN 1-895688-64-7 (bound) ISBN 1-895688-65-5 (pbk.)

1. Art – Technique – Juvenile literature.
2. Handicraft – Juvenile literature.
I. Title

N7430.W35 1997   j702'.8   C96-931441-8

Design & Art Direction: Julia Naimska

Art on the front cover, counterclockwise from upper left:
Batik Hanging and Easel; Squishy Sculpture; Chalk Creature; Lots of Dots; Styroblock Prints.

The crafts in this book have been tested and are safe when conducted as instructed.
The author and publisher accept no responsibility for any damage caused or sustained
by the use or misuse of ideas or material featured in the crafts in *I Can Make Art.*

Other books by Mary Wallace
I Can Make Toys
I Can Make Puppets
I Can Make Gifts
I Can Make Games
I Can Make Nature Crafts
I Can Make Costumes
I Can Make Jewelry
How to Make Great Stuff to Wear
How to Make Great Stuff for Your Room

Printed in Hong Kong

A   B   C   D   E   F

CONTENTS

Let's Make Art • *4*

You Can Make Art • *6*

Misty Morning • *8*

Picture Perfect • *10*

Tutti Frutti • *12*

Squishy Sculpture • *14*

Lots of Dots • *16*

Chalk Creature • *18*

Mosaic Magic • *20*

Styroblock Prints • *22*

Suncatcher • *24*

Kid-size Collage • *26*

Batik Hanging • *28*

Little Gallery • *30*

LET'S MAKE ART

You can make all the art in this book. It's easy. It's fun. These two pages show the things used to make everything here, but you can use other things if you like. You'll find most of what you need around the house — remember to get permission to use what you find and to display your art.

- cardboard
- tracing paper
- white paper
- tempera paint
- masking tape
- pencil
- play clay
- crayons
- soft paintbrush

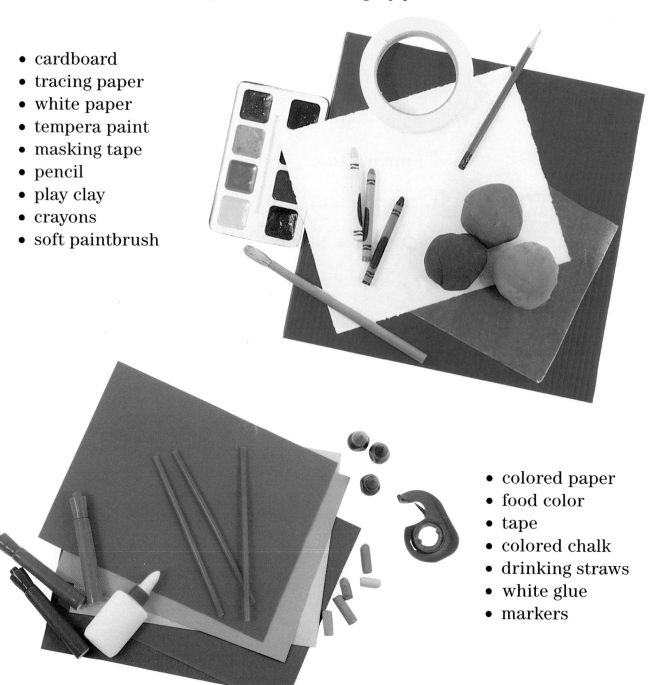

- colored paper
- food color
- tape
- colored chalk
- drinking straws
- white glue
- markers

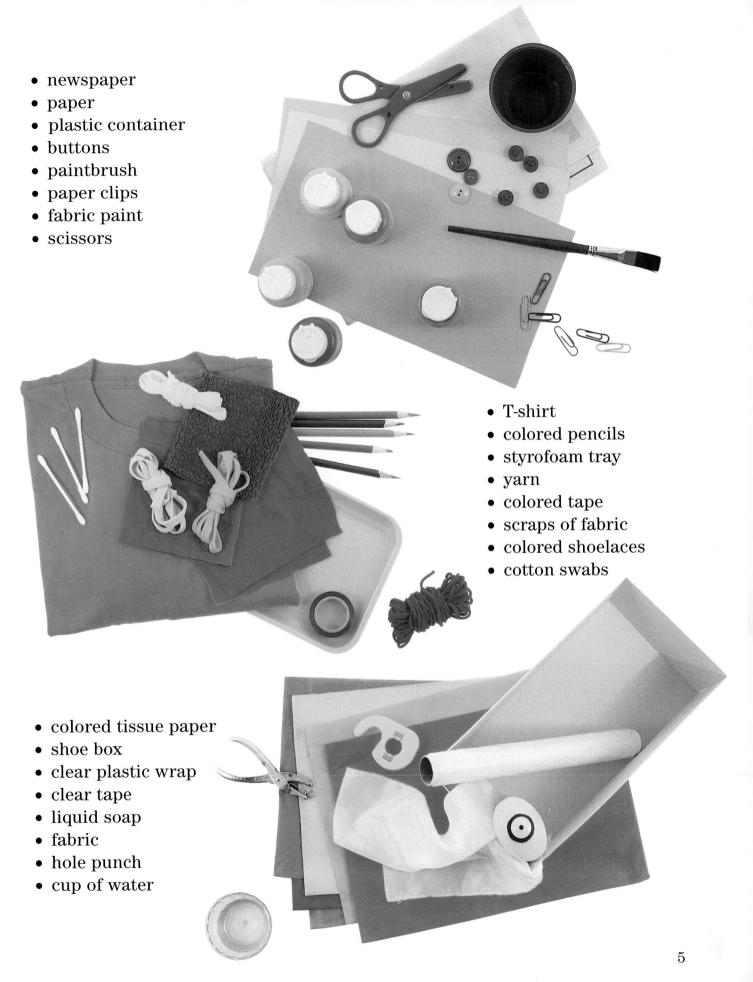

- newspaper
- paper
- plastic container
- buttons
- paintbrush
- paper clips
- fabric paint
- scissors

- T-shirt
- colored pencils
- styrofoam tray
- yarn
- colored tape
- scraps of fabric
- colored shoelaces
- cotton swabs

- colored tissue paper
- shoe box
- clear plastic wrap
- clear tape
- liquid soap
- fabric
- hole punch
- cup of water

YOU CAN MAKE ART

How do you see, feel and think about the world around you? When you make art, you express your world to other people.

You can make art that shows things exactly as you see them.

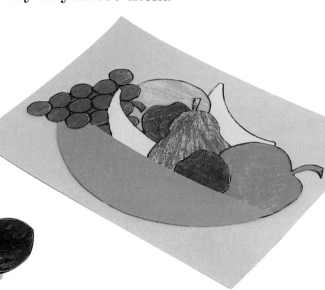

Or your art can show things as they are in your imagination.

Any way you feel can be shown in your art. It can be happy, sad, funny, exciting, calm, pretty or ugly. Here are some things you can use to make your art express what you feel:

color   *line*   *shape*   *pattern*   *texture*

Art is best when you share it with other people. This is called displaying your art.

Frame your pictures. Use a simple frame or add an extra frame called a mat. Then hang it for other people to see:

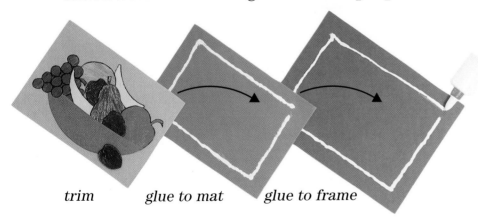   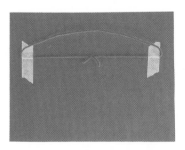

trim   *glue to mat*   *glue to frame*   *tape on yarn to hang*

Put your art on a card to give to a friend:

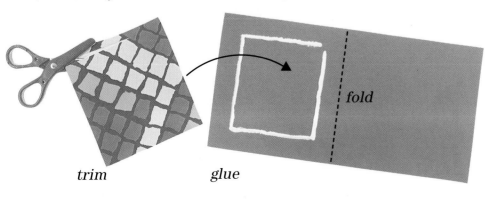   

trim   *glue*   *fold*

MISTY MORNING

- white paper
- masking tape
- water
- soft paintbrush
- tempera paint
- scissors

The colors in *watercolor* paints are mixed in water, so you can see the paper shining through the paint. When you paint with lots of water and a little paint, it is called a *wash*. A wash makes things look misty or far away, so it is good for painting *landscapes,* which are pictures of the outdoors.

1 tape paper to flat surface

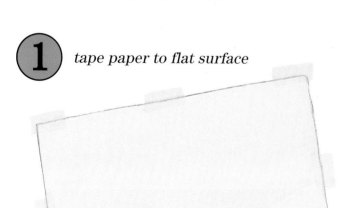

dip the brush in water and wet the whole paper

2 dip your brush in lots of
water and then a little paint

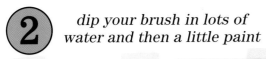

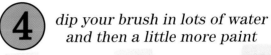

*paint a light
wash for sky and
water, and let dry*

3 dip your brush in lots of
water and then a little paint

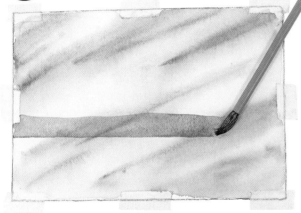

*paint a strip of wash
for hills far away, and let dry*

4 dip your brush in lots of water
and then a little more paint

*paint figures and water ripples
in the middle, and let dry*

5 use a wet brush with
lots of paint

paint the tree in the front, and let dry

6 remove tape

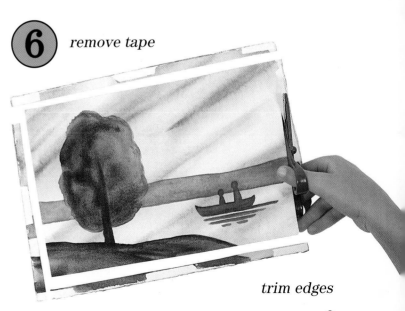

trim edges

For construction paper frame, see page 31.

PICTURE PERFECT

- paper
- paper clips
- pencil
- colored pencils

A *portrait* is a picture of a person. It can show the whole person or just the face. When you draw a portrait, be sure to include everything you notice about the person — color and length of hair, color and shape of eyes, if they have freckles or wear glasses . . .

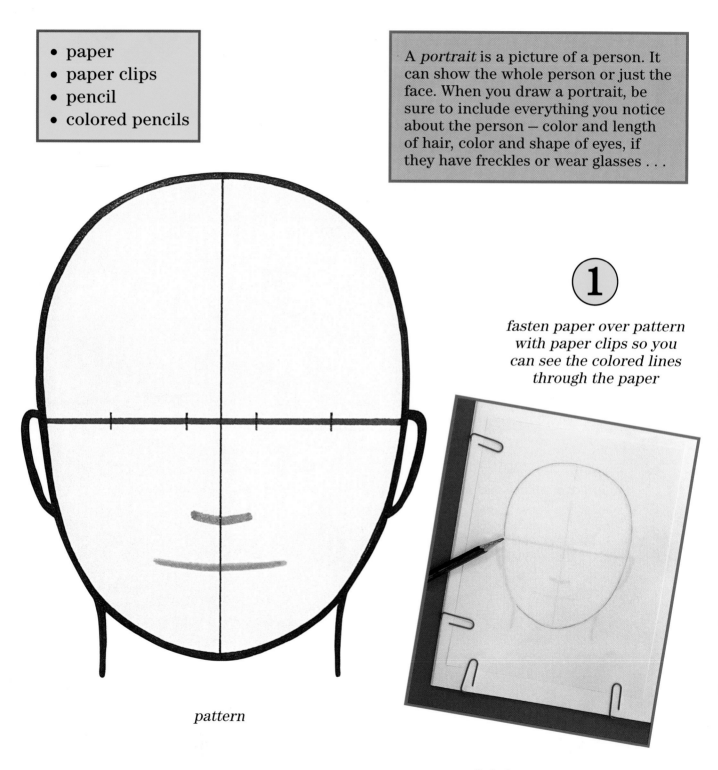

pattern

1

fasten paper over pattern with paper clips so you can see the colored lines through the paper

lightly trace the black oval shape and the neck

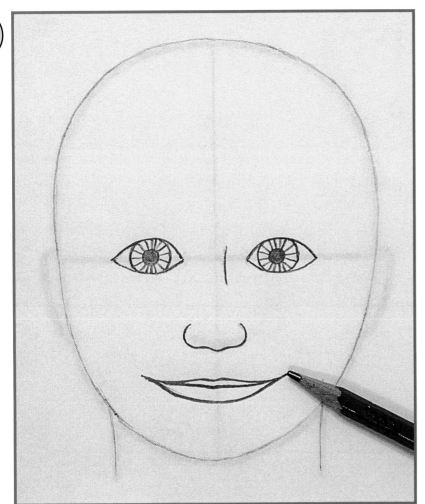

draw the eyes above
and below the blue line
as shown

draw the bottom of the
nose over the green line
as shown

draw the mouth above
and below the red line
as shown

lightly trace the ears

③

add lashes, lids
and brows to
the eyes

draw in the shapes
of the head, hair, ears, chin,
nose, neck and shoulders

④ color and shade with
colored pencils

TUTTI FRUTTI

COLOR WHEEL

- white paper circle
- pencil
- 3 crayons: yellow, blue and red

A *color wheel* shows you how colors combine to make other colors. You can make any color by mixing red, yellow and blue, the three *primary* colors. Mixing two primary colors makes one of the *secondary* colors: red + yellow = orange, yellow + blue = green, blue + red = purple.

1 divide circle into 6 sections

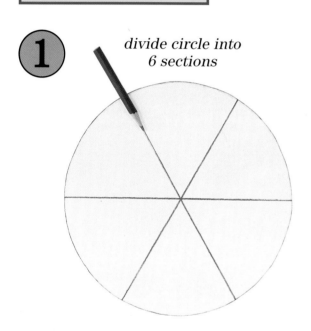

2 color 3 sections yellow as shown

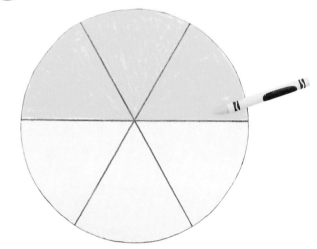
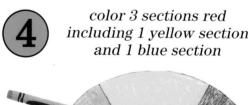

3 color 3 sections blue including 1 yellow section

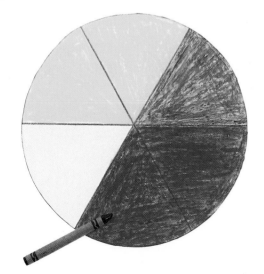

4 color 3 sections red including 1 yellow section and 1 blue section

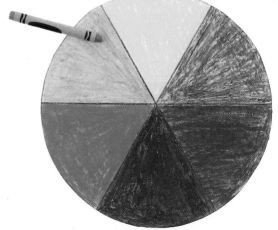

FUN WITH FRUIT

- color wheel
- pencil
- scissors
- construction paper
- white glue

 1 *add yellow to make orange and green brighter*

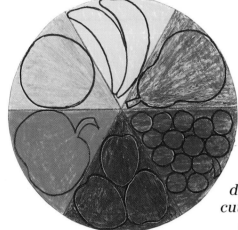

draw and cut out fruit shapes

A *still life* is a picture of things, just like a portrait is a picture of a person. A still life is often a picture of something very colorful, such as a bunch of flowers or a bowl of fruit.

2 *draw a bowl shape on construction paper and cut out*

3 *glue in place on paper*

For constuction paper frame, see page 31.   13

SQUISHY SCULPTURE

- plastic container
- play clay — bought or home-made

Sculpture is not flat like a drawing. A sculpture has a shape you can look at from any side, and you can feel it, too. Artists sculpt in all kinds of materials: stone, clay, metal, even cloth. After sculpting in your own play clay, try using plasticine or aluminum foil.

1 *make a ball of clay*

2 *flatten*

use as base for plastic container

3 *roll clay into balls and long pieces*

4 *gently wrap a long piece around the bottom of the container*

5 squish balls and strips
of clay in place

dabs of
water help
the clay stick
together

 **6** let finished sculpture dry
at least two days

MAKE YOUR OWN PLAY CLAY

1 Mix:
1 cup flour
1 cup salt
1/2 cup warm water
1 spoon alum
(available from drug store)
1 spoon cooking oil

2 divide into 3 batches and add a
different food color to each

3 knead until smooth

LOTS OF DOTS

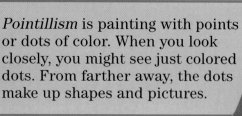

- plain T-shirt
- newspaper
- masking tape
- cotton swabs
- fabric paint

Pointillism is painting with points or dots of color. When you look closely, you might see just colored dots. From farther away, the dots make up shapes and pictures.

① *put layers of newspaper inside shirt so paint will not seep through*

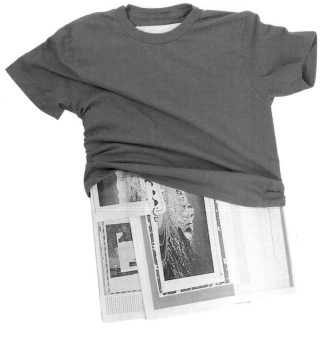

② *outline a shape in masking tape*

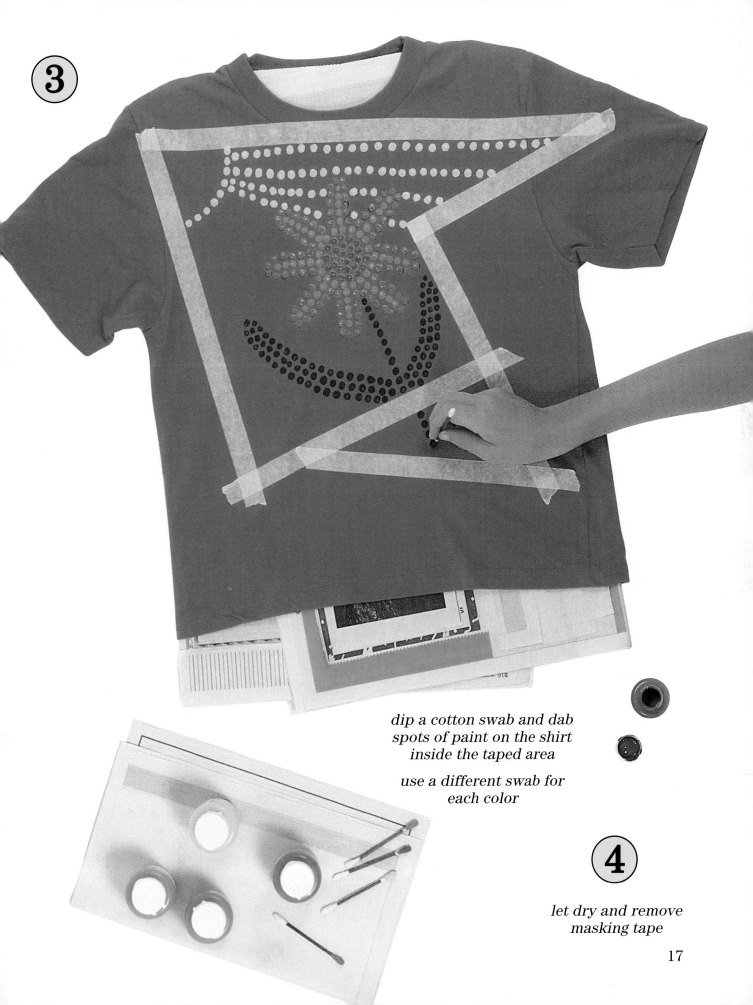

3

dip a cotton swab and dab
spots of paint on the shirt
inside the taped area

use a different swab for
each color

4

let dry and remove
masking tape

CHALK CREATURE

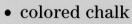

- colored chalk
- dark colored paper or a large rock or a piece of sidewalk
- scissors

People have made *chalk drawings* for a long, long time. In early times, people made chalk out of ground-up plants, charcoal or clay, and drew on bark, rocks or animal hides. They often drew real animals or creatures out of their imaginations.

draw a slightly curvy line for the back and tail of creature

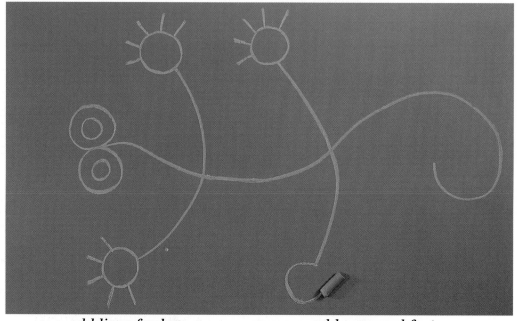

add lines for legs   *add eyes and feet*

2 *fill out the body using different colors and patterns then draw the outline of the creature's body*

dots

stripes

Xs

stars

spirals

circles

wavy lines

checkmarks

3 cut out creature drawn on paper and hang

For tape loops, see page 27.

MOSAIC MAGIC

- large corrugated cardboard box
- pencil
- scissors
- paint
- paintbrush
- colored paper
- white glue
- *grown-up to help*

 1 *have grown-up help you cut flaps and one side off the box*

paint and let dry

Mosaics are made from small pieces of just about anything — colored glass, stone, ceramic tile or paper — grouped together on a background. Mosaics decorate floors, walls, ceilings, screens, masks, pots, mirrors and more.

draw shapes along the top edge and cut

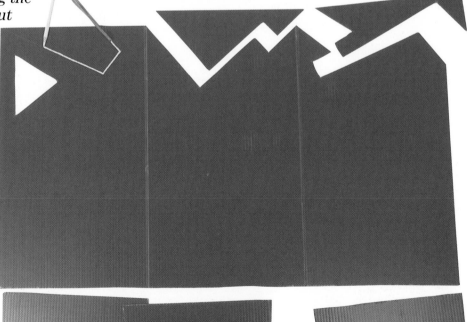

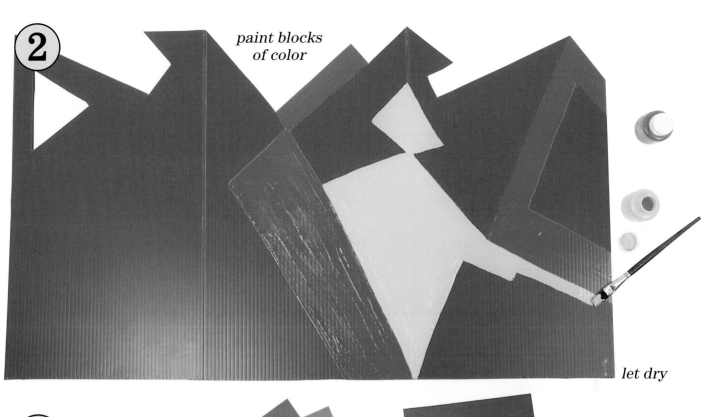

2

paint blocks
of color

let dry

3

tear colored paper
into small pieces

apply glue with
paintbrush

glue onto
cardboard

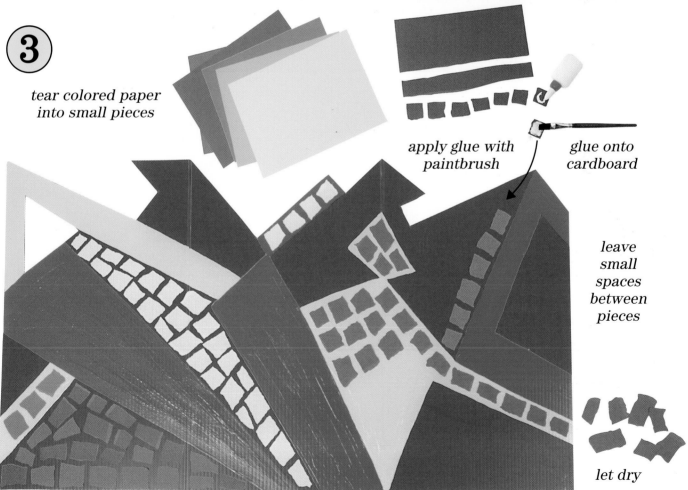

leave
small
spaces
between
pieces

let dry

fold slightly and stand upright

STYROBLOCK PRINTS

- styrofoam tray
- scissors
- pencil
- tempera paint and brush
- liquid soap
- different kinds of paper: paper bag, construction paper, etc.

Printmaking lets an artist make many copies of the same picture from one drawing. The drawing is carved into a *block* used to print copies onto paper. The print is the same as the drawing, only backwards!

(1) *trim edges off tray so it is flat*

(2) *draw a picture on the tray*

push pencil tip into the styrofoam along the lines

3

add a drop of
liquid soap to
paint so it sticks

paint over
picture

4 carefully place paper
on top and gently rub
paper agains paint

5

carefully lift
paper so ink
does not
smudge

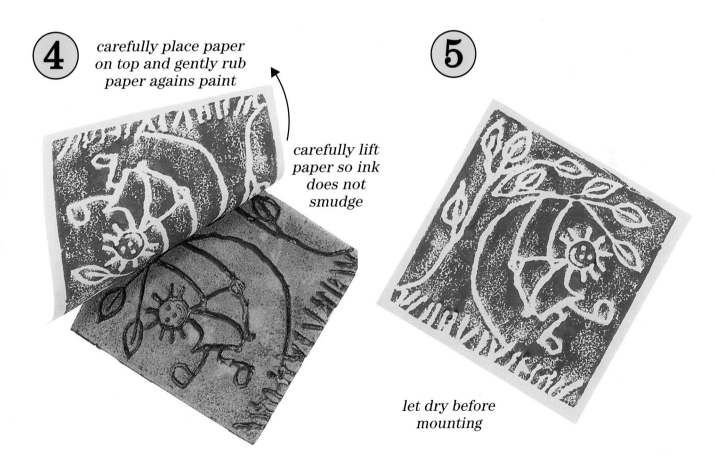

let dry before
mounting

For cards to mount prints on, see page 7.

SUNCATCHER

- cardboard
- pencil
- scissors
- clear plastic wrap
- clear tape
- colored tissue paper
- colored tape
- hole punch
- yarn
- *grown-up to help*

A suncatcher made from colored tissue paper and hanging in a window looks like *stained glass.* Stained glass is like a painting made of light. Pieces of colored glass are put together with metal strips in between. Sunlight shines through the glass, making it glow with light and color.

1 *draw a shape on cardboard and cut out*

2 *cut out center leaving a frame around the outside*

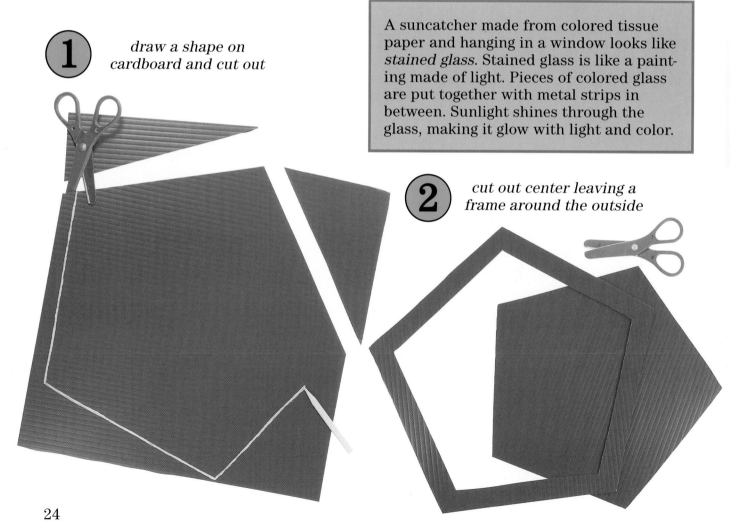

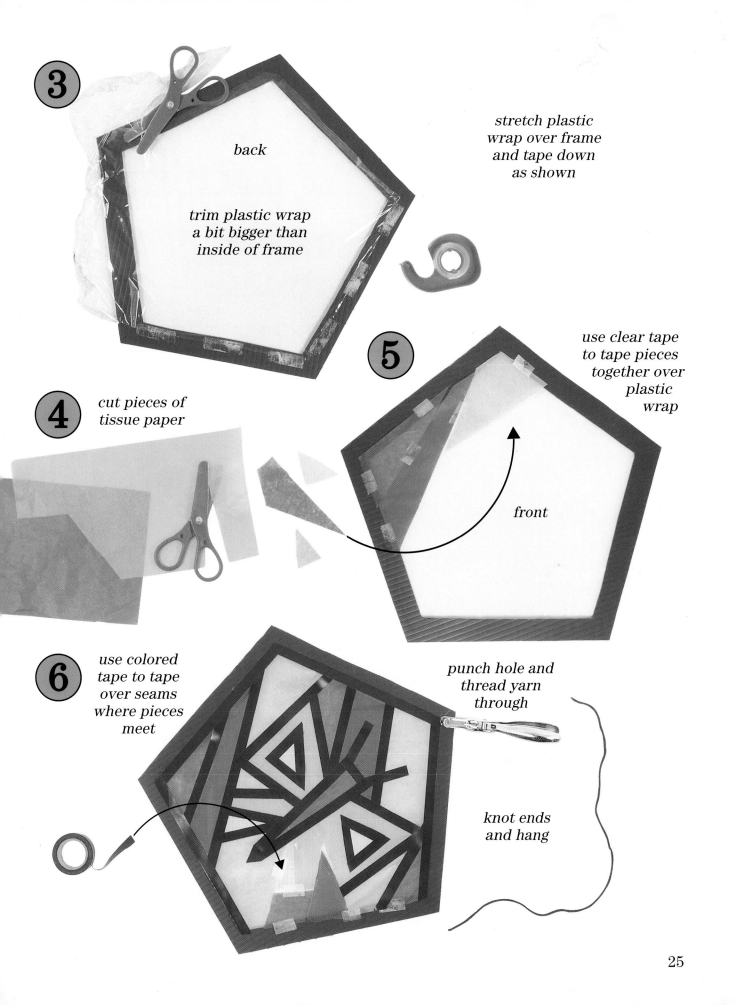

3

back

trim plastic wrap
a bit bigger than
inside of frame

stretch plastic
wrap over frame
and tape down
as shown

4 cut pieces of
tissue paper

5

use clear tape
to tape pieces
together over
plastic
wrap

front

6 use colored
tape to tape
over seams
where pieces
meet

punch hole and
thread yarn
through

knot ends
and hang

KID-SIZE COLLAGE

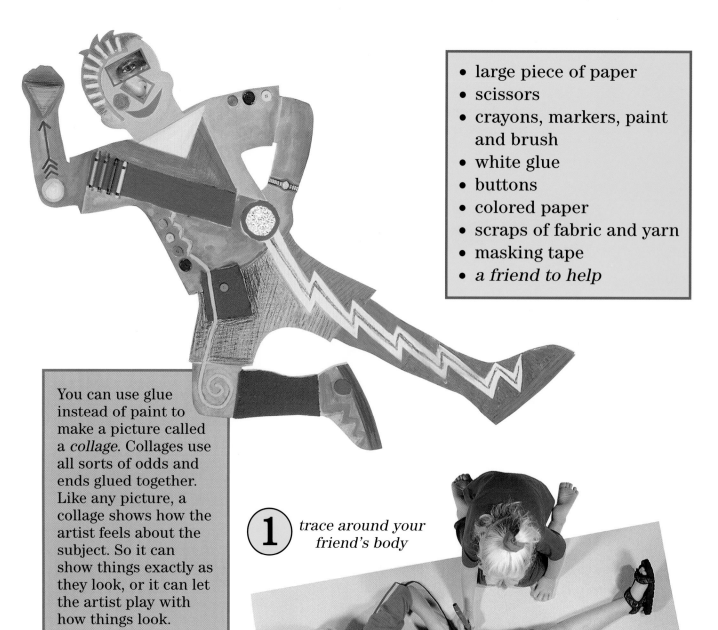

- large piece of paper
- scissors
- crayons, markers, paint and brush
- white glue
- buttons
- colored paper
- scraps of fabric and yarn
- masking tape
- *a friend to help*

You can use glue instead of paint to make a picture called a *collage*. Collages use all sorts of odds and ends glued together. Like any picture, a collage shows how the artist feels about the subject. So it can show things exactly as they look, or it can let the artist play with how things look.

1 *trace around your friend's body*

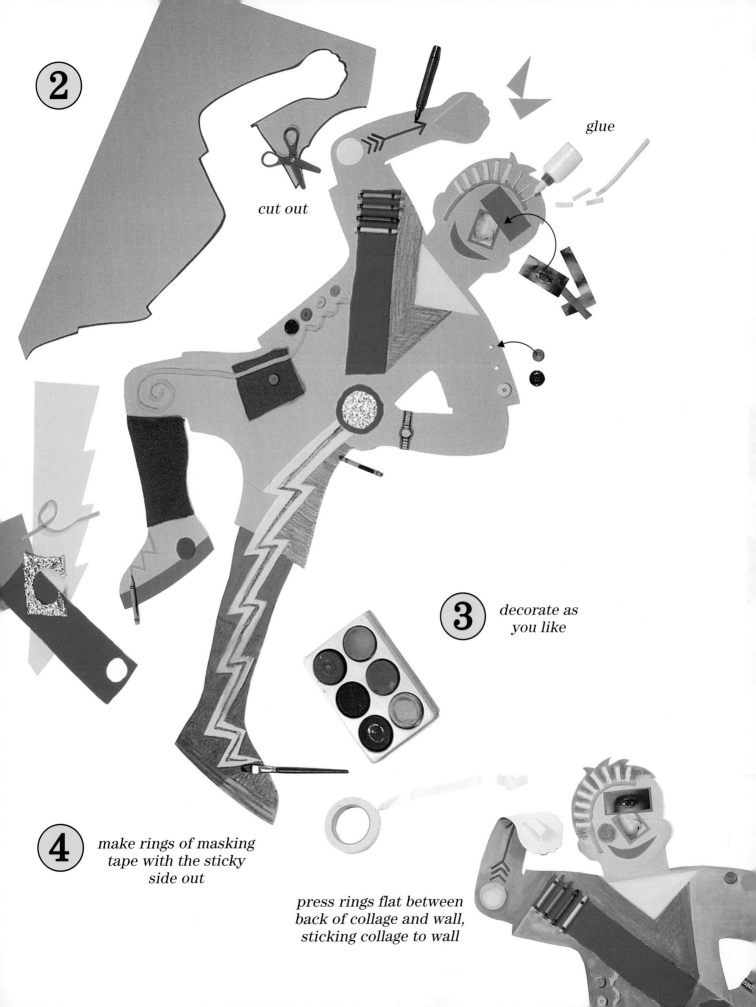

② cut out

glue

③ decorate as you like

④ make rings of masking tape with the sticky side out

press rings flat between back of collage and wall, sticking collage to wall

BATIK HANGING

- a piece of fabric that is narrower than a drinking straw
- crayons
- food color
- liquid soap
- bowl of water
- spoon
- 4 buttons
- paper clips
- 2 drinking straws
- white glue
- yarn

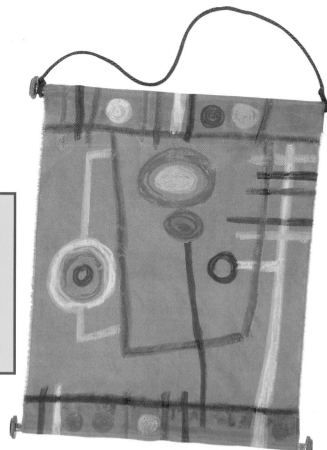

1

draw and color a design in crayon

Batik designs have been used to decorate cloth for a long, long time. Melted wax is painted on cloth. Then the cloth is dipped in colored dye. The dye sinks into the cloth everywhere but where the wax is.

2 *mix food color and a drop of liquid soap into the bowl of water*

28

3 *put cloth in and stir around*

4

5

unbend 4 paper clips and thread a button on each

lift out cloth and let water drip off

hang to dry

push a paper clip through each end of straw as shown, and repeat with second straw

6

place straw near end of cloth and fold end of cloth over straw

tie yarn ends to ends of one straw to make loop for hanging

glue down end of cloth

repeat with second straw

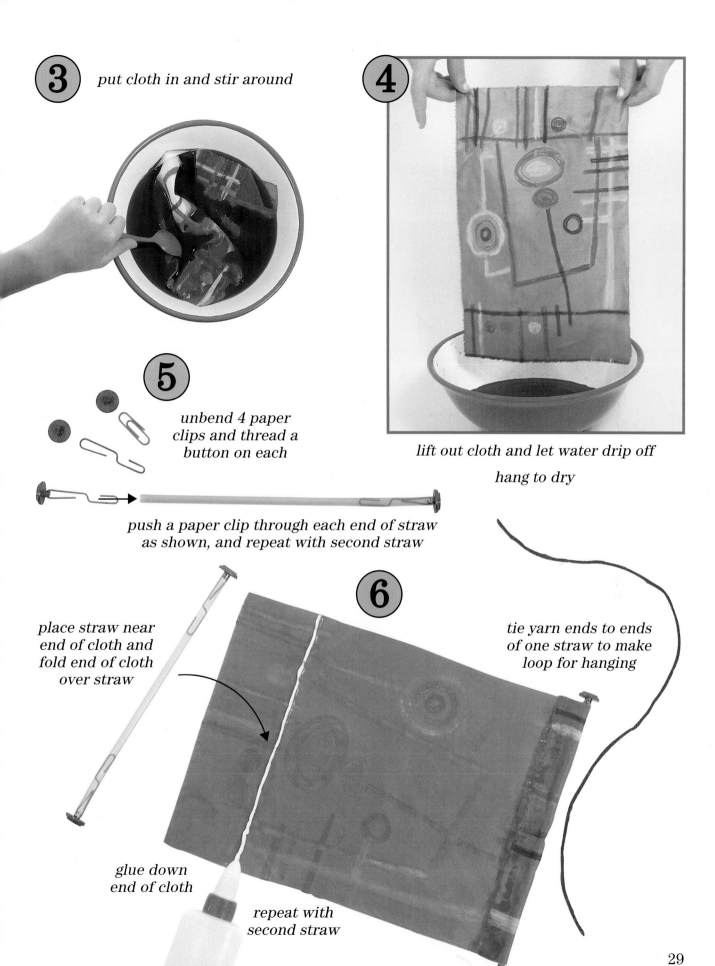

LITTLE GALLERY

An *art gallery* is a place to show art, sometimes in special shows called *exhibits*. An exhibit might show the work of one artist, or art that all has to do with a subject or *theme*. What theme do you think is shown here?

GALLERY

- shoe box
- scissors
- light colored paint
- paintbrush

1 cut off front of shoe box

paint and let dry

FRAME

- mini painting
- scissors
- construction paper
- white glue

1

trim edges of painting

2

glue back of painting

3

glue to piece of paper a little bigger than the painting

EASEL

- 2 drinking straws
- scissors
- tape

1

cut 1 straw in half

bend other straw as shown

2

tape 1 short piece across as shown

3

insert other short piece into bend and tape

trim so easel will lean back

To hang paintings, see page 7.   31

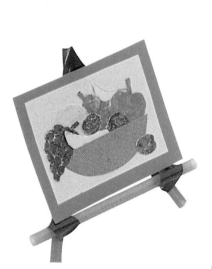

If you visit an art gallery, you can see all kinds of art — drawings, sculptures, paintings, photographs, and more. What kind of art do you like best? How does seeing art make you feel? People come to galleries to see and enjoy the ways that artists view their world. You can make your own art and your own gallery, where your friends and family will find their own favorites.